Born in 1956

By

Kerry Butters.

Born in 1956

Millennium: 2nd millennium

Centuries: 19th century – **20th century** – 21st century

Decades: 1920s 1930s 1940s – **1950s** – 1960s 1970s 1980s

Years: 1953 1954 1955 – **1956** – 1957 1958 1959

1956 (MCMLVI) was a leap year starting on Sunday (dominical letter AG) of the Gregorian calendar, the 1956th year of the Common Era (CE) and *Anno Domini* (AD) designations, the 956th year of the 2nd millennium, the 56th year of the 20th century, and the 7th year of the 1950s decade.

Contents

January

- January 1 – The Anglo-Egyptian Condominium ends in Sudan.
- January 3
    - By popular demand, *Peter Pan*, starring Mary Martin, is restaged live by Producers' Showcase on NBC-TV.
    - Columbia Records first releases Glenn Gould's solo piano recording of Bach's Goldberg Variations.
- January 8 – Operation Auca: Five U.S. evangelical Christian missionaries, Nate Saint, Roger Youderian, Ed McCully, Jim Elliot and Pete Fleming, are killed for trespassing by the Huaorani people of Ecuador shortly after making contact with them.
- January 16 – Egyptian leader Gamal Abdel Nasser vows to reconquer Palestine.
- January 25–26 – Finnish troops reoccupy Porkkala after Soviet troops vacate its military base. Civilians can return February 4.
- January 26 – The 1956 Winter Olympics open in Cortina d'Ampezzo, Italy.

February

- February 11 – British spies Guy Burgess and Donald Maclean resurface in the Soviet Union after being missing for 5 years.
- February 14–26 – 20th Congress of the Communist Party of the Soviet Union.
- February 16 – Only a little more than four months after the release of the 70mm version of *Oklahoma!*, the film version of Rodgers and Hammerstein's *Carousel*, starring Gordon MacRae and Shirley Jones, is released in CinemaScope 55. MacRae and Jones had previously starred in *Oklahoma! Carousel*, intended for showing in 55mm, ends up being shown only in 35mm.
- February 22 – Elvis Presley enters the United States music charts for the first time, with "Heartbreak Hotel".
- February 23 – Norma Jean Mortenson legally changes her name to Marilyn Monroe.
- February 24 – Doris Day records her most famous song, "Que Sera, Sera (Whatever Will Be, Will Be)"; it is from Alfred Hitchcock's *The Man Who Knew Too Much*, in which Day co-stars with James Stewart.
- February 25 – Nikita Khrushchev attacks the veneration of Joseph Stalin in a speech "On the Cult of Personality and Its Consequences".

March

- March 1 – The International Air Transport Association finalizes a draft of the radiotelephony spelling alphabet for the International Civil Aviation Organization.
- March 2 – Morocco declares its independence from France.
- March 9
  - The British deport Archbishop Makarios from Cyprus to the Seychelles.
  - Soviet Armed Forces suppresses mass demonstrations in the Georgian Soviet Socialist Republic, reacting to Nikita Khrushchev's de-Stalinization policy.
- March 10 – The Fairey Delta 2 broke the World Air Speed Record, raising it to 1,132 mph (1,811 km/h) or Mach 1.73, an increase of some 300 mph (480 km/h) over the previous record, and thus becoming the first aircraft to exceed 1,000 mph (1,600 km/h) in level flight.
- March 11 – After having opened in London the previous year, Laurence Olivier's film, *Richard III*, adapted from Shakespeare's play, has its U.S. premiere in theatres and on NBC Television on the same day. On TV it is not shown in prime time, but as an afternoon matinée, in a slightly cut version. It is one of the first such experiments of its kind. Olivier is later nominated for an Oscar for his performance.
- March 12
  - 96 U.S. Congressmen sign the Southern Manifesto, a protest against the 1954 Supreme Court ruling (*Brown v. Board of Education*) that desegregated public education.
  - The Dow Jones Industrial Average closes above 500 for the first time rising 2.40 points, or 0.48%, to 500.24.

- March 13 – Elvis Presley releases his first gold album titled *Elvis Presley*.
- March 15 – The Broadway musical *My Fair Lady* opens in New York City.
- March 19 – At age 48, Dutch boxer Bep van Klaveren contests his last match in Rotterdam.
- March 20 – Tunisia gains independence from France.
- March 21 – The 28th Academy Awards ceremony is held.
- March 23 – Pakistan becomes the first Islamic republic, and a national holiday is observed in the country including the former East Pakistan state.

April

A reel of 2-inch quadruplex videotape compared with a modern-day miniDV videocassette.

- April 2 – The first episode of *As the World Turns* is broadcast on the CBS television network in the United States.
- April 7 – Spain relinquishes its protectorate in Morocco.
- April 9 – Habib Bourguiba is elected President of the National Constituent Assembly of the Kingdom of Tunisia; on April 15 he becomes Prime Minister.

- April 14 – Videotape is first demonstrated at the 1956 NARTB (now NAB) convention in Chicago by Ampex. It is the demonstration of the first practical and commercially successful videotape format known as 2" Quadruplex.
- April 17 – Queen Elizabeth II inaugurates the 4.9 km² Chew Valley Lake in Somerset, England, as a reservoir for the Bristol area.
- April 18 – Maria Desylla-Kapodistria is elected mayor of Corfu and becomes the first female mayor in Greece.
- April 19
    - British diver Lionel Crabb (working for MI6) dives into Portsmouth harbour to investigate a visiting Soviet cruiser and vanishes.
    - American actress Grace Kelly marries Rainier III, Prince of Monaco.
- April 21 – Former U.S. First Daughter Margaret Truman marries Clifton Daniel.
- April 27 – Heavyweight boxing champion Rocky Marciano retires without losing a professional boxing match.

May

- May 2 – The United Methodist Church in America decides at its General Conference to grant women full ordained clergy status. It also calls for an end to racial segregation in the denomination.
- May 8
    - Austria and Israel form diplomatic relations.
    - The constitutional union between Indonesia and the Netherlands is dissolved.

- John Osborne's *Look Back in Anger* opens at the Royal Court Theatre, London, changing the scope of theatrical and other forms of drama in the UK: the theatre's press release describes the dramatist as among the angry young men of the time.
- May 9 – Manaslu, eighth highest mountain in the world, is first ascended.
- May 18 – Lhotse (main), the fourth highest mountain, is first ascended.
- May 23 – French minister Pierre Mendès France resigns due to his government's policy on Algeria.
- May 24 – The first Eurovision Song Contest is broadcast from Lugano, Switzerland. The winning song is the host country's *Refrain* by Lys Assia (music by Géo Voumard, text by Émile Gardaz).
- May 25 – India announces the institution of diplomatic relations with Spain (still under Franco's rule)

June

- June 1 – Vyacheslav Molotov resigns as foreign minister of the Soviet Union; he later becomes ambassador in Mongolia.
- June 3 – British Rail renames 'Third Class' passenger facilities as 'Second Class' (Second Class facilities had been abolished in 1875, leaving just First Class and Third Class).
- June 5 – Elvis Presley performs "Hound Dog", on *The Milton Berle Show*, scandalizing the audience with his suggestive hip movements.

- June 6 – In Singapore, chief minister David Marshall resigns after the breakdown of talks about internal self-government in London.
- June 8 – General Electric/Telechron introduces model 7H241 "The Snooz Alarm", first snooze alarm clock ever.
- June 10 – 1956 Summer Olympics: Equestrian events open in Stockholm, Sweden (all other events are held in November in Melbourne, Australia).
- June 13
  - International Criminal Police Organization (ICPO).
  - Real Madrid beats Stade Reims 4-3 at Parc des Princes, Paris and wins the 1955–56 European Cup (football).
- June 14 – The Flag of the United States Army is formally dedicated.
- June 15 – Eindhoven University of Technology is founded in Eindhoven, The Netherlands.
- June 18 – The last foreign troops leave Egypt.
- June 21 – Playwright Arthur Miller appears before the House UnAmerican Activities Committee.
- June 23 – Gamal Abdel Nasser becomes the 2nd president of Egypt.
- June 28
  - MP Sydney Silverman's bill for the abolition of the death penalty in the UK passes the British House of Commons.
  - Labour riots in Poznań, Poland, are crushed with heavy loss of life. Soviet troops fire at a crowd protesting high prices, killing 53 people.
  - The film version of Rodgers and Hammerstein's *The King and I*, starring Deborah Kerr and Yul Brynner, is

released only a few months after the film version of R&H's *Carousel*. It becomes the most financially successful film version of a Rodgers and Hammerstein musical up to that time, and the only one to win an acting Oscar (Yul Brynner wins Best Actor for his performance as the King of Siam). It is also one of two Rodgers and Hammerstein films to be nominated for Best Picture (which it does not win).

- June 29
  - Actress Marilyn Monroe marries playwright Arthur Miller.
  - President Dwight D. Eisenhower signs the Federal Aid Highway Act, creating the Interstate Highway System.
- June 30 – A TWA Lockheed Constellation and United Airlines Douglas DC-7 collide in mid-air over the Grand Canyon in Arizona, killing all 128 people aboard both aircraft in the deadliest civil aviation disaster to date; the accident leads to sweeping changes in the regulation of cross-country flight and air traffic control over the United States.

July

- July 2 – A lab experiment involving scrap thorium at Sylvania Electric Products in Bayside, New York, results in an explosion.
- July 4 – The first Lockheed U-2 spy plane flight over the Soviet Union.

- July 8 – The mountain Gasherbrum II, on the border of Pakistan and China, is first ascended by an Austrian expedition.
- July 10 – The British House of Lords defeats the abolition of the death penalty.
- July 16 – With the closing of its "Big Tent" show in Pittsburgh, Ringling Bros. and Barnum & Bailey Circus announces all subsequent circuses will be "arena shows" due to changing economics.
- July 24 – At New York City's Copacabana nightclub, Dean Martin and Jerry Lewis perform their last comedy show together (their act started on July 25, 1946).
- July 25 – The Italian ocean liner SS *Andrea Doria* sinks after colliding with the Swedish ship SS *Stockholm* in heavy fog 72 kilometers (45 mi) south of Nantucket island, killing 51.
- July 26 – Egyptian leader Gamal Abdel Nasser nationalizes the Suez Canal sparking international condemnation.
- July 30 – A joint resolution of Congress is signed by President Dwight D. Eisenhower, authorizing "In God we trust" as the U.S. national motto.
- July 31 – Cricket: Jim Laker sets an extraordinary record at Old Trafford in the fourth Test between England and Australia, taking 19 wickets in a first class match (the previous best was 17).

August

- August 6 – After going bankrupt in 1955, the American broadcaster DuMont Television Network airs its final broadcast, an episode of its sports series *Boxing from St. Nicholas Arena*.

- August 8 – 262 miners die in a fire in a coal mine in Marcinelle, Belgium.
- August 9 – The exhibition *This Is Tomorrow* opens at Whitechapel Art Gallery in London.
- August 12 – Around 5,000 members of the Romanian Greek-Catholic Church hold a mass outside Cluj-Napoca Piarists' Church to demonstrate that their church, proscribed by the government in 1948, has not ceased to exist as the regime claims.
- August 17 – West Germany bans the Communist Party of Germany.

September

- September 9 – Elvis Presley appears on *The Ed Sullivan Show* for the first time.
- September 13 – The hard disk drive is invented by an IBM team led by Reynold B. Johnson.
- September 16 – Television broadcasting commences in Australia.
- September 21 – Nicaraguan dictator Anastasio Somoza García is assassinated.
- September 25 – The submarine transatlantic telephone cable opens.
- September 27 – The Bell X-2 becomes the first manned aircraft to reach Mach 3.

October

- October 5 – Cecil B. DeMille's epic film *The Ten Commandments*, starring Charlton Heston as Moses, is released in the United States. It will be in the top ten of the worldwide list of highest-grossing films of all time adjusted for inflation.
- October 8 – Baseball pitcher Don Larsen of the New York Yankees throws the only perfect game in World Series history in Game 5 of the 1956 World Series against the Brooklyn Dodgers. Yogi Berra catches the game. Dale Mitchell is the final out. The New York Yankees win the series. Larsen is named series MVP.
- October 10
  - Finland joins UNESCO.
  - The prototype Lockheed L-1649 Starliner, the final Lockheed Constellation model, makes its first flight.
- October 14
  - Indira Kala Sangeet University, Khairagarh is inaugurated by Prime Minister of India Indira Gandhi.
  - Dalit Buddhist movement: Dr. B. R. Ambedkar, Indian Dalit leader, converts to Buddhism along with 385,000 followers.
- October 15 – The British Royal Air Force retires its last Avro Lancaster bomber.
- October 17
  - The world's first commercial nuclear power plant is opened at Calder Hall in England.

- The Game of the Century (chess): 13-year-old Bobby Fischer beats grandmaster Donald Byrne in the Rosenwald Memorial Tournament in New York City.
- October 22 – Suez Crisis: The United Kingdom, France, and Israel secretly meet in and make plans to invade Egypt.
- October 23 – Hungarian Revolution breaks out against the pro-Soviet government, originating as a student demonstration in Budapest. Hungary attempts to leave the Warsaw Pact.
- October 26 – Red Army troops invade Hungary.
- October 29
  - Suez Crisis: Israel invades the Sinai Peninsula and pushes Egyptian forces back toward the Suez Canal.
  - Tangier Protocol: The international city Tangier is reintegrated into Morocco.
  - The *Huntley-Brinkley Report* debuts on NBC-TV in the United States.
- October 31
  - Suez Crisis: The United Kingdom and France begin bombing Egypt to force the reopening of the Suez Canal.
  - A United States Navy team becomes the third group to reach the South Pole (arriving by air) and commences construction of the first permanent Amundsen–Scott South Pole Station.

November

- November 1
  - The States Reorganisation Act of India reforms the boundaries and names of Indian states. Two new states Kerala and Karnataka were formed.
  - City Lights Books publishes *Howl and Other Poems* by Allen Ginsberg.
  - The film *Oklahoma!* (1955), previously released to select cities in Todd-AO, now receives a national release in CinemaScope, since not all theatres are yet equipped for Todd-AO. To accomplish this, the film had to be actually shot twice, rather than printing one version in two different film processes as is done today.
- November 3 – MGM's film *The Wizard of Oz* is the first major Hollywood film running more than ninety minutes to be televised uncut in one evening.
- November 4 – 1956 Hungarian Revolution: More Soviet troops invade Hungary to crush a revolt that started on October 23. Thousands are killed, more are wounded, and nearly a quarter million leave the country.
- November 6 – United States presidential election, 1956: Republican incumbent Dwight D. Eisenhower defeats Democrat challenger Adlai E. Stevenson in a rematch of their contest 4 years earlier.
- November 7 – Suez Crisis: The United Nations General Assembly adopts a resolution calling for the United Kingdom, France, and Israel to withdraw their troops from Arab lands immediately.

- November 13 – The United States Supreme Court declares illegal the state and municipal laws requiring segregated buses in Montgomery, Alabama, thus ending the Montgomery Bus Boycott.
- November 12 – Born in Brazil Lucia Regina D'Acri.
- November 14 – Fighting ends in Hungary.
- November 15 – Middle East Technical University is founded in Ankara, Turkey.
- November 18 – At the reception of the Polish embassy in Moscow Nikita Khrushchev uttered his famous phrase "We will bury you".
- November 20 – In Yugoslavia, former prime minister Milovan Đilas is arrested after he criticizes Josip Broz Tito.
- November 22 – The 1956 Summer Olympics begin in Melbourne, Australia.
- November 23 – The Suez Crisis causes petrol rationing in Britain.
- November 25 – Fidel Castro and Che Guevara depart from Tuxpan, Veracruz, Mexico, en route to Santiago de Cuba aboard the yacht *Granma* with 82 men.
- November 28 – Roger Vadim's drama film *And God Created Woman*, released in France as *Et Dieu . . . créa la femme*, propels Brigitte Bardot into the public spotlight as a "sex kitten".
- November 30 – Floyd Patterson wins the world heavyweight boxing championship that was vacant after the retirement of Rocky Marciano.

December

- December 2
  - Fidel Castro and his followers land in Cuba in the boat *Granma*.
  - A pipe bomb planted by George Metesky explodes at the Paramount Theater in Brooklyn, injuring 6 people.
- December 3 – 1956 Bush Terminal explosion in Brooklyn
- December 4 – The Million Dollar Quartet (Elvis Presley, Jerry Lee Lewis, Carl Perkins, and Johnny Cash) get together at Sun Studio for the first and last time in history.
- December 5 – Rose Heilbron becomes Britain's first female judge.
- December 9 – Trans-Canada Air Lines Flight 810 crashes into a mountain in British Columbia. All 62 people on board are killed.
- December 12 – Japan becomes a member of the United Nations.
- December 18 – *To Tell the Truth* debuts on CBS-TV.
- December 19 – John Bodkin Adams is arrested for the murder of 2 patients in Eastbourne, Great Britain.
- December 23 – British and French troops leave the Suez Canal region.
- December 31 – Bob Barker makes his TV debut as host of the game show *Truth or Consequences*.

Date unknown

- Asian flu pandemic originates in China.
- Minamata disease is discovered.

Births

January

Mel Gibson

David Caruso

Bill Maher

Geena Davis

Mimi Rogers

Johnny Rotten

- January 1
  - Mark R. Hughes, American entrepreneur (d. 2000)
  - Kōji Yakusho, Japanese actor
  - Christine Lagarde, French lawyer and politician
  - Andrew Lesnie, Australian cinematographer (d. 2015)
- January 3

- Mel Gibson, American actor and director
- Tomiko Suzuki, Japanese voice actress (d. 2003)
- January 5
  - Celso Blues Boy, Brazilian singer and guitarist (d. 2012)
  - Chen Kenichi, Japan-born Chinese chef
  - Frank-Walter Steinmeier, German politician
- January 7
  - David Caruso, American actor (*NYPD Blue*)
  - Uwe Ochsenknecht, German actor
  - Johnny Owen, Welsh professional boxer (d. 1980)
- January 9
  - Kimberly Beck, American actress
  - Imelda Staunton, English actress
- January 14 – Ronan Bennett, Northern Irish writer
- January 16 – Martin Jol, Dutch football manager
- January 17 – Paul Young, English musician
- January 18 – Tom Bailey, English musician
- January 19 – Adriana Acosta, Argentine militant and field hockey player
- January 20 – Bill Maher, American actor, comedian, and political analyst
- January 21 – Geena Davis, American actress
- January 24 – Lounès Matoub, Algerian Berber Kabyle singer
- January 25 – Bronwyn Pike, Australian politician
- January 27
  - Susanne Blakeslee, American actress
  - Mimi Rogers, American actress
- January 28 – Peter Schilling, German singer
- January 29
  - Jan Jakub Kolski, Polish film director

- ○ Irlene Mandrell, American musician, actress
- January 31 – Johnny Rotten, British punk musician and TV personality

February

Nathan Lane

Jay Nixon

- February 1 – Mike Kitchen, Canadian ice hockey player and coach
- February 2 - Philip Franks, English actor and director
- February 3
  - ○ Nathan Lane, American actor
  - ○ Lee Ranaldo, American musician
- February 6 – Jon Walmsley, British actor
- February 10 – Enele Sopoaga, Tuvaluan politician and diplomat

- February 11
  - Catherine Hickland, American actress
  - Didier Lockwood, French jazz violinist
- February 13
  - Yiannis Kouros, Greek-Australian ultra marathoner
  - Jay Nixon, 55th Governor of Missouri
  - Paul Stojanovich, American television producer
- February 14 – Tom Burlinson, Australian actor
- February 15 – Desmond Haynes, West Indian cricketer
- February 18 – Thomas Gradin, Swedish hockey player
- February 19
  - Kathleen Beller, American actress
  - Roderick MacKinnon, American biologist, recipient of the Nobel Prize in Chemistry
  - Dave Wakeling, English musician
- February 23
  - Reinhold Beckmann, German television presenter
- February 24
  - Judith Butler, American philosopher
  - Paula Zahn, American television journalist
- February 25
  - Davie Cooper, Scottish footballer (d. 1995)
  - Michel Friedman, German lawyer, politician and talk show host
- February 26 – Michel Houellebecq, French author
  - Keisuke Kuwata, Japanese musician
- February 29
  - Mike Compton, American mandolinist
  - Bob Speller, Canadian politician
  - Aileen Wuornos, American serial killer (d. 2002)

March

Bryan Cranston

Catherine Ashton

José Manuel Barroso

- March 1
  - Tim Daly, American screen actor
  - Dalia Grybauskaitė, President of Lithuania
- March 2 – Eduardo Rodríguez, President of Bolivia
- March 5
  - Teena Marie, American singer (d. 2010)
  - Marco Paolini, Italian stage actor, dramaturge and author
- March 7 – Bryan Cranston, American actor
- March 11 – Rob Paulsen, American voice actor
- March 13 – Dana Delany, American actress

- March 16 – Vladimír Godár, Slovak composer
- March 18 – Ingemar Stenmark, Swedish alpine skier
- March 19 – Yegor Gaidar, Russian economist and politician
- March 20
  - Catherine Ashton, British politician
  - Naoto Takenaka, Japanese actor, comedian, singer and director
- March 21
  - José Manuel Barroso, Prime Minister of Portugal
  - Ingrid Kristiansen, Norwegian runner
  - Win Lyovarin, Thai author
- March 24 – Steve Ballmer, CEO of Microsoft (2000–2014)
- March 28
  - Susan Ershler, American mountaineer
  - Evelin Jahl, German athlete
- March 29 – Evie, American Christian musician
- March 30 – Shahla Sherkat, Iranian feminist journalist

April

Andy García

Lars von Trier

- April 3
    - Ray Combs, American game show host and comedian (d. 1996)
    - Boris Miljković, Serbian TV & theatre director and video artist
- April 4
    - Kerry Chikarovski, Australian politician
    - David E. Kelley, American writer and television producer
- April 5 – Diamond Dallas Page, former American professional wrestler
- April 6
    - Sebastian Spreng, American-Argentinean visual artist
    - Dilip Vengsarkar, Indian cricketer
- April 12
    - Andy García, Cuban-American actor
    - Herbert Grönemeyer, German musician and actor
    - Yasuo Tanaka, Japanese politician, novelist
- April 13 – Possum Bourne, New Zealand rally car driver (d. 2003)
- April 14 – Barbara Bonney, American soprano

- April 16
  - David McDowell Brown, American astronaut (*Columbia Disaster*) (d. 2003)
  - Lise-Marie Morerod, Swiss skier
- April 18
  - John James, American actor
  - Melody Thomas Scott, American actress
- April 19 – Sue Barker, British tennis player and television presenter
- April 21 – Phillip Longman, American demographer
- April 22 – Jukka-Pekka Saraste, Finnish conductor
- April 26 – Koo Stark, British actress
- April 28 – Hanka Paldum, Bosnian singer
- April 30 – Lars von Trier, Danish film director

May

Jan Peter Balkenende

- May 1 – Alexander Ivanov, Russian-born American chess grandmaster
- May 4
  - David Guterson, American writer
  - Ulrike Meyfarth, German high jumper

- May 5 – Lisa Eilbacher, American actress
- May 6 – Vladimir Lisin, Russian business oligarch
- May 7
  - Jan Peter Balkenende, Prime Minister of the Netherlands
  - Jean Lapierre, Canadian politician and television host
- May 9 – Wendy Crewson, Canadian actress
- May 10 – Vladislav Nikolayevich Listyev, Russian journalist (d. 1995)
- May 13
  - Kenneth Eriksson, Swedish rally driver
  - Sri Sri Ravi Shankar, Indian guru
  - Kirk Thornton, American voice actor
- May 15 – Dan Patrick, American sports commentator
- May 17
  - Sugar Ray Leonard, African American boxer
  - Bob Saget, American actor and television host
- May 20
  - Ingvar Ambjørnsen, Norwegian author
  - Dean Butler, American actor and producer
- May 23
  - Ursula Plassnik, Austrian politician
  - Buck Showalter, American baseball player and manager
- May 24 – Michael Jackson, Irish Anglican bishop
- May 26 – Lisa Niemi, American actress and dancer, widow of Patrick Swayze
- May 28
  - Jerry Douglas, American dobro player
  - John O'Donoghue, former Irish Fianna Fáil politician

- ○ Sayuri Yamauchi, Japanese voice actress (d. 2012)
- May 29 – La Toya Jackson, African-American singer
- May 31 – Yoshiko Sakakibara, Japanese voice actress

June

Björn Borg

Chris Isaak

- June 3 – George Burley, Scottish football manager
- June 5 – Kenny G, American saxophonist
- June 6 – Björn Borg, Swedish tennis player
- June 7 – Antonio M. Reid, American record executive
- June 8 – Udo Bullmann, German politician
- June 9 – Patricia Cornwell, American novelist
- June 10 – Borwin, Duke of Mecklenburg, German head of the House of Mecklenburg
- June 11
  - ○ Joe Montana, American football player
  - ○ Arthur Porter, Canadian physician (d. 2015)
- June 14 – King Diamond, Danish heavy metal musician

- June 15 – Robin Curtis, American actress
- June 17 – Andrew Bicknell, English actor
- June 20 – Cho Chikun, Korean professional Go player
- June 23 – Randy Jackson, African American musician and talent judge
- June 25
  - Anthony Bourdain, American chef, author and television personality
  - Boris Trajkovski, President of the Republic of Macedonia (d. 2004)
  - Chloe Webb, American actress and singer
- June 26 – Chris Isaak, American musician
- June 27 – Heiner Dopp, German field hockey player
- June 28 – Noel Mugavin, Australian rules football player

July

Tom Hanks

Sela Ward

- July 1 – Alan Ruck, American actor
- July 2 – Jerry Hall, American model and actress
- July 3 – Rick Ducommun, Canadian actor and comedian
- July 5 – Sheila Walsh, Scottish Christian artist and former talk-show hostess
- July 9 – Tom Hanks, American actor and director
- July 11
  - Amitav Ghosh, Indian-American fiction writer
  - Sela Ward, American actress
- July 12 – Mel Harris, American actress
- July 13 – Günther Jauch, German television host
- July 14 – Vladimir Kulich, Czech actor
- July 15
  - Ian Curtis, English rock musician (Joy Division) (d. 1980)
  - Barry Melrose, Canadian hockey player, coach, and commentator
  - Toshihiko Seko, Japanese long-distance runner
- July 16 – Tony Kushner, American playwright
- July 18 – Sheila Aldridge, American singer
- July 19 – Yoshiaki Yatsu, Japanese professional wrestler
- July 24

- o Charlie Crist, American politician
- o Pat Finn, American game show host and producer
- o Carmen Nebel, German television presenter
- July 26
  - o Andy Goldsworthy, British sculptor and photographer
  - o Dorothy Hamill, American figure skater and Olympic Gold medalist
- July 30 – Delta Burke, American actress
- July 31
  - o Michael Biehn, American actor
  - o Deval Patrick, American politician; first African-American Governor of Massachusetts

August

Bruce Greenwood

Kim Cattrall

- August 2 – Jim Neidhart, American professional wrestler
- August 4 – Gerry Cooney, American boxer
- August 5
  - Ferdi Bolland, Dutch musician, songwriter, and music producer (Bolland & Bolland)
  - Maureen McCormick, American actress
- August 6 – Stepfanie Kramer, American actress
- August 7 – Ernie Johnson, Jr., American sportscaster
- August 8 – Chris Foreman, English rock guitarist
- August 10
  - Fred Ottman, American professional wrestler
  - Charlie Peacock, American Christian producer, singer-songwriter
- August 12 – Bruce Greenwood, Canadian actor
- August 14
  - Jackée Harry, American actress and television personality
  - Rusty Wallace, American NASCAR race car driver
- August 17 – Dave Jones, English football manager
- August 19 – Adam Arkin, American actor
- August 20 – Joan Allen, American actress
- August 21 – Kim Cattrall, English-born Canadian actress
- August 22 – Paul Molitor, American baseball player
- August 23 – Andreas Floer, German mathematician (d. 1991)
- August 24 – John Culberson, American politician
- August 26 – Mark Mangino, American football coach
- August 29 – Mark Morris, American choreographer
- August 31
  - Masashi Tashiro, Japanese television performer
  - Tsai Ing-wen, Taiwanese president

September

David Copperfield

Leslie Cheung

Linda Hamilton

- September 1 – Bernie Wagenblast, American editor and broadcaster
- September 2 – Angelo Fusco, Provisional Irish Republican Army member
- September 3 – Pat McGeown, Provisional Irish Republican Army member (d. 1996)
- September 11 – Phillip D. Bissett, American politician

- September 12
    - Leslie Cheung, Hong Kong actor (d. 2003)
    - Ricky Rudd, American race car driver
    - Walter Woon, law professor and former Nominated Member of Parliament and Attorney-General of Singapore
- September 14
    - Kostas Karamanlis, Greek politician
    - Ray Wilkins, English footballer and coach
- September 15 – George Howard, American jazz saxophone musician (d. 1998)
- September 16
    - Sergei Beloglazov, Russian free-style wrestler
    - David Copperfield, American illusionist
- September 17 – Brian Andreas, American writer, sculptor, painter, and publisher
- September 18 – Tim McInnerny, English actor
- September 20
    - Gary Cole, American actor
    - Debbi Morgan, African-American actress
- September 21 – Jack Givens, American basketball player
- September 23 – Paolo Rossi, Italian soccer player
- September 24 – Gregory Peter Panos, American futurist, writer, inventor
- September 25 – Jamie Hyneman, American television co-host
- September 26 – Linda Hamilton, American actress
- September 29 – Sebastian Coe, Baron Coe, British athlete; co-ordinator of the London 2012 Olympic Games
- September 30 – Gordon Elliott, British-Australian television personality and talk show host

October

Christoph Waltz

Martina Navratilova

Mahmoud Ahmadinejad

- October 1
  - Tara Buckman, American actress
  - Andrus Ansip, Prime Minister of Estonia
- October 2- Charlie Adler, American voice actor and director
- October 3 – Ralph Morgenstern, German actor
- October 4 – Christoph Waltz, German-Austrian actor

- October 8 – Stephanie Zimbalist, American actress
- October 10 – Amanda Burton, Irish actress
- October 11 – Nicanor Duarte, President of Paraguay
- October 12 – Trần Đại Quang, President of Vietnam
- October 16 – Rudra Mohammad Shahidullah, Bangladeshi poet (d. 1992)
- October 17 – Mae Jemison, African American astronaut
- October 18 – Martina Navratilova, Czech-American tennis player
- October 19 – Carlo Urbani, Italian physician (d. 2003)
- October 20 – Danny Boyle, English film director
- October 21 – Carrie Fisher, American actress
- October 23 – Dwight Yoakam, American country singer, musician and actor
- October 26 – Rita Wilson, American actress and producer
- October 28 – Mahmoud Ahmadinejad, 6th President of Iran

November

Richard Curtis

Bo Derek

- November 5 – Rob Fisher, British keyboardist and songwriter (Climie Fisher) (d. 1999)
- November 8 – Richard Curtis, English film director, producer and screenwriter
- November 10 – Mohsen Badawi, Egyptian entrepreneur, political activist, and writer
- November 14 – Avi Cohen, Israeli football player (d. 2010)
- November 17 – Kelly Ward, American actor
- November 18
  - Noel Brotherston, Irish footballer (d. 1995)
  - Warren Moon, American football player
- November 20
  - Bo Derek, American actress and model
  - Olli Dittrich, German actor, comedian, television personality and musician
- November 21 – Terri Welles, American actress and adult model
- November 23
  - Shane Gould, Australian swimmer
  - Nikolay Sidorov, Soviet athlete

- Jimmy Hibbert, British comedian and script writer and script editor
- November 24 – Jouni Kaipainen, Finnish composer
- November 26 – Dale Jarrett, American race car driver
- November 27 – William Fichtner, American actor
- November 28
  - Kristine Arnold, American singer (Sweethearts of the Rodeo)
  - Lucy Gutteridge, English actress
- November 29
  - Eric Laakso, American football player
  - Leo Laporte, American author and television host

December

- December 5
  - Klaus Allofs, German football player
  - Krystian Zimerman, Polish pianist
- December 6 – Randy Rhoads, American Guitarist (d. 1982)
- December 7
  - Larry Bird, American basketball player
  - Iveta Radičová, Prime Minister of Slovakia
- December 9 – Jean-Pierre Thiollet, French writer
- December 11 – Lani Brockman, American playwright
- December 12
  - Ana Alicia, Mexican actress
  - Johan van der Velde, Dutch cyclist
- December 13 – Majida El Roumi, Lebanese singer
- December 14 – Béla Réthy, German sports journalist
- December 16 – Duncan Faure, South African musician

- December 18 – Ron White, American comedian
- December 19
  - Masami Akita, Japanese noise musician (also known as Merzbow)
  - Jimmy Cauty, British musician (The KLF, The Timelords)
- December 21 – Anna Erlandsson, Swedish filmmaker and animator
- December 23 – Michele Alboreto, Italian race car driver (d. 2001)
- December 26 – David Sedaris, American essayist
- December 28
  - Nigel Kennedy, English violinist
  - Jimmy Nicholl, Canadian-born footballer
- December 29 – Fred MacAulay, Scottish comedian
- December 30
  - Patricia Kalember, American actress
  - Sheryl Lee Ralph, African American actress
- December 31 – Hussein Ahmed Salah, Djiboutian marathon player

Date unknown

- Gilma Jiménez, Colombian politician (d. 2013)
- Nancy Lynn, American aerobatic pilot (d. 2006)
- Shelagh Rogers, Canadian radio host
- Miladin Šobić, Montenegrin singer
- Susan Solomon, American atmospheric chemist

Deaths

January

Irène Joliot-Curie

- January 3
    - Alexander Gretchaninov, Russian composer (b. 1864)
    - Joseph Wirth, Chancellor of Germany (b. 1876)
- January 5 – Mistinguett, French singer (b. 1875)
- January 9 – Marion Leonard, American actress (b. 1881)
- January 12 – Norman Kerry, American actor (b. 1894)
- January 13 – Lyonel Charles Feininger, German painter (b. 1871)
- January 14 – Sheila Kaye-Smith, English writer (b. 1887)
- January 18 – Konstantin Päts, President of Estonia (b. 1874)
- January 21 – Sam Langford, Canadian boxer (b. 1883)
- January 24 – Sir Alexander Korda, Hungarian-born film director (b. 1893)
- January 27 – Erich Kleiber, German conductor (b. 1890)
- January 29 – H. L. Mencken, American writer (b. 1880)
- January 31 – A. A. Milne, English author (*Winnie The Pooh*) (b. 1882)

February

Heinrich Barkhausen

- February 2
  - Bob Burns, American comedian (b. 1890)
  - Charles Grapewin, American actor (b. 1869)
- February 8 – Connie Mack, American baseball executive and manager (Philadelphia Athletics) and a member of the MLB Hall of Fame (b. 1862)
- February 10 – Hugh Trenchard, 1st Viscount Trenchard, British marshal of the Royal Air Force (b. 1873)
- February 18 – Gustave Charpentier, French composer (b. 1860)
- February 20
  - Heinrich Barkhausen, German physicist (b. 1881)
  - James Cousins, Irish writer (b. 1873)
- February 26 – Elsie Janis, American singer and actress (b. 1889)
- February 29 – Elpidio Quirino, President of the Philippines (b. 1890)

March

- March 14 – David Browning, American Olympic diver (b. 1931)
- March 17
  - Fred Allen, American comedian (b. 1894)

- o Irène Joliot-Curie, French physicist, recipient of the Nobel Prize in Chemistry (b. 1897)
- March 18 – Louis Bromfield, American writer (b. 1896)
- March 20
  - o Fanny Durack, Australian swimmer (b. 1889)
  - o Wilhelm Miklas, Austrian politician and 3rd President of Austria
- March 25
  - o Lou Moore, American racing driver and team owner (b. 1904)
  - o Robert Newton, English film actor (b. 1905)
- March 28 – Thomas de Hartmann, Russian composer (b. 1885)
- March 30 – Edmund Clerihew Bentley, English inventor (b. 1875)
- March 31 – Ralph DePalma, Italian-born race car driver (b. 1884)

April

Alben W. Barkley

- April 6 – Pío Valenzuela, Filipino physician and one of the leaders of the Katipunan (b. 1869)
- April 13 – Emil Nolde, German-Danish painter (b. 1867)

- April 15 – Kathleen Howard, Canadian-born American actress and opera singer (b. 1884)
- April 19 – Ernst Robert Curtius, Alsatian philologist (b. 1886)
- April 21
  - Samuel Gottesman, American pulp-paper merchant (b. 1885)
  - Charles MacArthur, American playwright and screenwriter (b. 1895)
- April 24 – Henry Stephenson, British character actor (b. 1871)
- April 26 – Edward Arnold, American actor (b. 1890)
- June 28 – Friedrich Schmidt-Ott, German lawyer, scientific organizer, and science policymaker (b. 1860)
- April 29
  - Harold Bride, English-born junior radio officer on RMS *Titanic* (b. 1890)
  - Wilhelm Ritter von Leeb, German field marshal (b. 1876)
- April 30 – Alben W. Barkley, 35th Vice President of the United States (b. 1877)

May

- May 3
  - Rodney Collin, British writer (b. 1909)
  - Peter Watson, English art collector and benefactor (b. 1908)
- May 12 – Louis Calhern, American actor (b. 1895)
- May 17 – Austin Osman Spare, English magician (b. 1886)
- May 18 – Maurice Tate, English cricketer (b. 1895)
- May 20

- ○ Max Beerbohm, English theater critic (b. 1872)
- ○ Zoltán Halmay, Hungarian Olympic swimmer (b. 1881)
- May 23 – Gustav Suits, Estonian poet (b. 1883)
- May 24 – Guy Kibbee, American actor (b. 1882)
- May 26 – Al Simmons, American baseball player (Philadelphia Athletics) and a member of the MLB Hall of Fame (b. 1902)
- May 29 – Frank Beaurepaire, Australian Olympic swimmer (b. 1891)
- May 31 – Diedrich Hermann Westermann, German linguist (b. 1875)

June

- June 2
- ○ Richard S. Edwards, American admiral (b. 1885)
- ○ Jean Hersholt, Danish actor (b. 1886)
- June 4 – Katherine MacDonald, American silent film actress (b. 1891)
- June 6 – Margaret Wycherly, English stage and film actress (b. 1881)
- June 11 – Ralph Morgan, American actor (b. 1883)
- June 17 – Paul Rostock, German official, surgeon, and university professor (b. 1892)
- June 22 – Walter de la Mare, English poet, short story writer, and novelist (b. 1873)
- June 23 – Reinhold Glière, Russian composer (b. 1875)
- June 26 – Clifford Brown, American jazz trumpeter (b. 1930)

July

- July 7 – Gottfried Benn, German poet (b. 1886)
- July 8 – Giovanni Papini, Italian essayist, poet, novelist (b. 1881)
- July 10 – Joe Giard, American baseball player (b. 1898)
- July 11 – John T. Raulston, Scopes Monkey Trial judge (b. 1868)
- July 20 – James Alexander Calder, Canadian politician (b. 1868)

August

Bertolt Brecht

Alfred Kinsey

- August 2 – Albert Woolson, last surviving Union veteran of the American Civil War (b. 1847)
- August 11 – Jackson Pollock, American painter (b. 1912)

- August 14
  - Bertolt Brecht, German playwright (b. 1898)
  - Konstantin von Neurath, Nazi German diplomat and foreign minister (b. 1873)
- August 16
  - Bela Lugosi, Hungarian-born film actor (*Dracula*) (b. 1882)
  - Lynde D. McCormick, American admiral (b. 1895)
- August 23 – Peaches Browning, American actress (b. 1910)
- August 24 – Kenji Mizoguchi, Japanese film director (b. 1898)
- August 25 – Alfred Kinsey, American sex researcher (b. 1894)

September

Billy Bishop

- September 6 – Lee Jung-seob, Korean oil painter (b. 1916)
- September 11 – Billy Bishop, Canadian World War I flying ace (b. 1894)
- September 20 – Flora Eldershaw, Australian novelist, critic, and historian (b. 1897)
- September 22 – Frederick Soddy, English chemist, Nobel Prize laureate (b. 1877)

- September 27
    - Milburn G. Apt, American test pilot (b. 1924)
    - Babe Zaharias, American golfer (b. 1911)
- September 29 – Anastasio Somoza García, President of Nicaragua (b. 1896)

October

Juho Kusti Paasikivi

- October 1 – Albert Von Tilzer, American songwriter (b. 1878)
- October 2 – George Bancroft, American actor (b. 1882)
- October 9 – Marie Doro, American stage & silent film actress (b. 1882)
- October 12 – Don Lorenzo Perosi, Italian composer (b. 1872)
- October 17 – Anne Crawford, British actress (b. 1920)
- October 19 – Isham Jones, American musician (b. 1894)
- October 22 – Hannah Mitchell, English socialist and suffragette (b. 1872)
- October 25 – Risto Ryti, 5th President of Finland (b. 1889)
- October 26 – Walter Gieseking, French conductor (b. 1895)

November

- November 1 – Pietro Badoglio, Italian general and prime minister (b. 1871)
- November 5 – Art Tatum, American jazz pianist (b. 1909)
- November 6 – Paul Kelly, stage and film actor (b. 1899)
- November 10
    - Harry F. Sinclair, American entrepreneur (b. 1876)
    - Victor Young, American composer (b. 1900)
- November 14 – Peter R. de Vries, Dutch crime reporter (b. 1956)
- November 19 – Francis L. Sullivan, English actor (b. 1903)
- November 22 – Theodore Kosloff, Russian-born ballet dancer, choreographer and actor (b. 1882)
- November 24 – Guido Cantelli, Italian conductor (b. 1920)
- November 26 – Tommy Dorsey, American trombonist and bandleader (b. 1905)
- November 27 – Hugo Ballin, American artist, film production designer, and director (b. 1879)

December

- December 2 – Dell Henderson, Canadian actor (b. 1883)
- December 6 – Dr B. R. Ambedkar, A founding father of modern India, the architect of its constitution and Indian dalit leader (b. 1891)
- December 7 – Huntley Gordon, Canadian actor (b. 1887)
- December 10 – David Shimoni, Israeli poet and writer (b. 1891)

- December 14 – Juho Kusti Paasikivi, 7th President of Finland (b. 1870)
- December 16 – Nina Hamnett, Welsh artist (b. 1890)
- December 17 – Eddie Acuff, American actor (b. 1903)
- December 26 – Holmes Herbert, English actor (b. 1882)
- December 30 – Ruth Draper, American actress (b. 1884)

Date unknown

- Lotte Herrlich, female photographer of German naturism

Nobel Prizes

- Physics – William Shockley, John Bardeen, Walter Houser Brattain
- Chemistry – Sir Cyril Norman Hinshelwood, Nikolay Semyonov
- Physiology or Medicine – André Frédéric Cournand, Werner Forssmann, Dickinson W. Richards
- Literature – Juan Ramón Jiménez
- Peace – Not Awarded

In the News.

Suez Crisis causes petrol rationing in Britain.

Switzerland wins the first Eurovision song contest.

Prince Ranier of Monaco marries Grace Kelly.

US Carries Out H Bomb Tests Bikini Atoll.

Elvis Presley releases his first hit.

The hovercraft was invented by Christopher Cockerell.

1956 Most Popular TV shows:

1. I Love Lucy (CBS)
2. The Ed Sullivan Show (CBS)
3. General Electric Theatre (CBS)
4. The $64,000 Question (CBS)
5. December Bride (CBS)
6. Alfred Hitchcock Presents (CBS)
7. I've Got A Secret (CBS)
8. Gunsmoke (CBS)
9. The Perry Como Show (NBC)
10. The Jack Benny Show (CBS)

1956 Calendar

January 1956
Sun	Mon	Tue	Wed	Thu	Fri	Sat
1	2	3	4	5	6	7
8	9	10	11	12	13	14
15	16	17	18	19	20	21
22	23	24	25	26	27	28
29	30	31				

February 1956
Sun	Mon	Tue	Wed	Thu	Fri	Sat
			1	2	3	4
5	6	7	8	9	10	11
12	13	14	15	16	17	18
19	20	21	22	23	24	25
26	27	28	29			

March 1956
Sun	Mon	Tue	Wed	Thu	Fri	Sat
				1	2	3
4	5	6	7	8	9	10
11	12	13	14	15	16	17
18	19	20	21	22	23	24
25	26	27	28	29	30	31

April 1956
Sun	Mon	Tue	Wed	Thu	Fri	Sat
1	2	3	4	5	6	7
8	9	10	11	12	13	14
15	16	17	18	19	20	21
22	23	24	25	26	27	28
29	30					

May 1956
Sun	Mon	Tue	Wed	Thu	Fri	Sat
		1	2	3	4	5
6	7	8	9	10	11	12
13	14	15	16	17	18	19
20	21	22	23	24	25	26
27	28	29	30	31		

June 1956
Sun	Mon	Tue	Wed	Thu	Fri	Sat
					1	2
3	4	5	6	7	8	9
10	11	12	13	14	15	16
17	18	19	20	21	22	23
24	25	26	27	28	29	30

July 1956
Sun	Mon	Tue	Wed	Thu	Fri	Sat
1	2	3	4	5	6	7
8	9	10	11	12	13	14
15	16	17	18	19	20	21
22	23	24	25	26	27	28
29	30	31				

August 1956
Sun	Mon	Tue	Wed	Thu	Fri	Sat
			1	2	3	4
5	6	7	8	9	10	11
12	13	14	15	16	17	18
19	20	21	22	23	24	25
26	27	28	29	30	31	

September 1956
Sun	Mon	Tue	Wed	Thu	Fri	Sat
						1
2	3	4	5	6	7	8
9	10	11	12	13	14	15
16	17	18	19	20	21	22
23	24	25	26	27	28	29
30						

October 1956
Sun	Mon	Tue	Wed	Thu	Fri	Sat
	1	2	3	4	5	6
7	8	9	10	11	12	13
14	15	16	17	18	19	20
21	22	23	24	25	26	27
28	29	30	31			

November 1956
Sun	Mon	Tue	Wed	Thu	Fri	Sat
				1	2	3
4	5	6	7	8	9	10
11	12	13	14	15	16	17
18	19	20	21	22	23	24
25	26	27	28	29	30	

December 1956
Sun	Mon	Tue	Wed	Thu	Fri	Sat
						1
2	3	4	5	6	7	8
9	10	11	12	13	14	15
16	17	18	19	20	21	22
23	24	25	26	27	28	29
30	31					

www.thepeoplehistory.com

www.ingramcontent.com/pod-product-compliance
Lightning Source LLC
Chambersburg PA
CBHW071132280526
45787CB00003B/1252